Considerations
on the Assassination *of*
Gérard Lebovici

GUY DEBORD

First published in French in 1985 by Gérard Lebovici

©Gallimard 1993
©TamTam Books 2001
Introduction and Translation by Robert Greene ©2001
First published by TamTam Books in the U.S.A. 2001

This work, published as part of a program of aid for publication, received support
from the French Ministry of Foreign Affairs and the Cultural Services of the French
Embassy in the United States.

Cet ouvrage, publié dans le cadre d'un programme d'aide à la publication, bénéficie
du soutien du Ministère des Affaires étrangères et du Service Culturel de
l'Ambassade de France aux Etats-Unis.

TamTam Books wants to thank Ichiro Shimizu, John McHale, Dominique Forma,
Christiaan van Bremen, Merril Greene and Jennifer Wei Leung for their wisdom and
assistance on this project.

TamTam Books is edited and published by Tosh Berman.

TamTam Books are designed by Tom Recchion.

TamTam Books
2601 Waverly Drive
Los Angeles, CA 90039-2724

Tosh@loop.com
www.tamtambooks.com

First Edition
ISBN 0-9662346-2-6

Library of Congress Control Number: 2001089199

Guy Debord

Considerations on the Assassination of Gérard Lebovici

(Considérations sur l'assassinat de Gérard Lebovici)

Translated from the French and Introduction by Robert Greene

BOOKS

©2001

*And when luck will have it that the people no longer have any
confidence in anybody, as sometimes happens, having been deceived
in the past by things or by men, what necessary befalls is ruin.*

(Machiavelli)

On March 5, 1984, Gérard Lebovici—one of France's biggest film producers at the time, and head of Champ Libre, a publishing house which printed revolutionary tracts and literary classics—received a curious phone call while at his film offices near the Champs Elysées. The caller said that he was phoning on behalf of Sabrina Mesrine. Sabrina was the daughter of France's former public enemy number one, Jacques Mesrine, who had been killed in a police ambush in 1979. While in prison, Mesrine had written a book called *The Death Instinct* in which he expressed his utter disdain for society as it was and for the police who maintained the order of such a society. The police had brought pressure on the Ministry of Justice, obscure laws were enforced, and the original publisher of the book was forced to take it out of circulation. Gérard Lebovici had republished *The Death Instinct* in early 1984 and had also become the adopted father to Sabrina. After he received the phone call that afternoon, purportedly on behalf of Sabrina, Lebovici canceled several appointments, notified his wife that he would be home late, then left his office at around 6:30 pm.

Early in the morning of March 7, he was found dead behind the steering wheel of his Renault in an underground parking lot, four bullet wounds in the back of his head. The gun that was used was the most nondescript possible, the hardest to trace. No money was taken, only Lebovici's identity papers. In his pocket was a note with the name "François" on it. The assassination had the markings of a cleverly planned ambush. The police considered several possibilities. The film business in France had become increasingly infiltrated by the Mafia, which was also involved in the burgeoning video piracy business. Perhaps Lebovici had resisted the Mafia's advances, and this was its response. The police also looked into Lebovici's purported connections with violent elements of the far left, and in particular his relationship with Guy Debord, one of the founders of the Situationist International and Lebovici's close friend. Perhaps Lebovici had refused to fund a particular subversive group and was made to pay the price. It was also possible that the perpetrator was an underworld friend or rival of Mesrine's who resented Lebovici's involvement in the Mesrine affair.

As soon as the assassination became public, the press ran wild with all kinds of stories. A portrait was painted of a man who, on the one hand, hobnobbed with Catherine Deneuve, on the other with Guy Debord, the notorious subversive whose works were published by Champ Libre. Those journalists mildly on the left theorized that Debord had slowly isolated Lebovici from his friends, transformed him into a hardcore situationist, with all of the dangers that would entail. The growing estrangement from his professional milieu and his involvement in extreme political activities might have led him into something he would regret, as he fell under the spell of Debord. On the right, the tendency was to look at Lebovici's supposed funding of left-wing terrorist organizations. The assassination was a settling of accounts. For several weeks, the public feasted on speculations concerning Debord's control over Lebovici, even his responsibility for the crime. The police only seemed to encourage such speculations, since they had not only questioned Debord as part of their investigation, but had revealed parts of the dossier on him—gathered over the years by French intelligence—to the press.

Seventeen years later, the crime remains unsolved. The speculations about terrorist groups or Mafia involvement led nowhere. The case is closed. According to Edgar Allan Poe's literary detective, C. Auguste Dupin, there are two ways to go in solving a supposed mystery. First, look at what precisely has occurred that has not occurred before, what stands out from the ordinary, what gives the event a peculiar quality. Second, enter the mind of the perpetrator, go through the various mental sequences he would consider before committing the crime. In the Lebovici case, what first stands out are the various enigmas that seem deliberate—the call made purportedly on behalf of Sabrina; the theft of the murdered man's identification papers (for what purpose?); the note from "François," an extremely common French name. What also stands out is the lack of any reverberations from the crime. One would expect more assassinations within the film world, sudden power moves here and there filling up the vacuum after Lebovici's death. But there were no subsequent events in the film or publishing worlds, or from within Lebovici's business to indicate that it had come from any such direction. In other words, the perpetrators had made the circumstances and the assassination unreadable. They kept perfect silence. That was not the sign of a typical Mafia hit, or a settling of accounts among terrorists, or the moves of a business rival.

And what about the thought processes of the assassins? They were clearly men who planned their ambush well. And such plans must have included consideration of the assassination's aftermath, as played out in the press. Lebovici had made numerous enemies; more importantly, Debord's uncompromising critiques of society, his disdain for all those who make a living within such a society, and most assuredly for any journalist, made him a man with few allies anywhere. If the assassination were done in a unreadable manner, stirring suspicion in many directions, some kind of suspicion would almost naturally fall on Debord. The press would home in on the sensational aspect—Lebovici's supposed double life, Debord's apparent secretiveness, certainly an indication of some kind of guilt.

While all of this went on, few in the press or public would bother to look in those directions that were actually more logical, in other words in the actual direction of the perpetrators. Such directions could include the extreme right wing, several factions of which had ample reason to hate Lebovici and wish him dead. (The assassination had occurred on the anniversary of Stalin's death, with the killers perhaps trying to link the two men.) It could also include the police itself, elements of which had a pathological hatred of Mesrine and who could not have looked too kindly on Lebovici for his republishing of *The Death Instinct*. (When Sabrina Mesrine had first been called in by the police to receive the news of her father's death, the police chief greeted her with a full glass of champagne in his hand.) It could also include a combination of several interests—business, law enforcement, political—who counted on the silence or collusion of others. "It is becoming more difficult to apply the principle *Cui prodest*? [who benefits by this?] in a world where so many acting interests are so well hidden. And so, within the integrated spectacle, one lives and dies at the point of confluence of a great number of mysteries." (Debord) In any event, the diversion and ambiguity worked to perfection.

The Lebovici case points to a possible ominous trend within the spectacle. Modern society is organized around secrecy and uncertainty. It is hard to fathom where certain interests lie, what groups have influence over others. We do not know where our food comes from, what regulates the prices of certain commodities, what intricate network of international companies produces the most commonplace object. The public is mostly in the dark, dependent on the press for what is considered news. They are vulnerable to suggestion and bouts of hysteria. Those who wish to do away with someone or gain greater influence in such a society can use this to great advantage. If a criminal deed needs doing, deliberately leave clues that are mysterious and unreadable. The press will then do much of the subsequent work for you, publishing speculative stories that have entertainment value and little rational content. Amidst such confusion, traces are lost, false leads are pursued. Furthermore, anyone who tries to solve the mystery, to inject some rationality in the discussion seems to be a conspiracy theorist, yet another paranoid type babbling about UFO cover-ups, a United Nations takeover, etc.

The spectacle has entered a phase of hyper-irrationality. "The lack of logic, namely the loss of the possibility of instantaneously distinguishing between what is important and what is unimportant or not a part of the question; what is incompatible or inversely what is relevant; everything that is implied by a particular consequence and everything that is also not implied; this disease has been voluntarily injected in large doses into the population by the anesthetists-resuscitators of the spectacle." (Debord) And there is no more effective anesthetist than the media, which thrives in an environment of increasing illiteracy. The newspaper articles that Debord quotes in *Considerations* provide a veritable primer on modern illogic, and include tactics that are used almost daily by the press.

The most widespread tactic is the *petitio principii*, otherwise known as begging the question. A completely false premise—for instance, situationists have ties to terrorist organizations—is reported as fact, and from that false premise all kinds of grand and entertaining conclusions can be drawn. This might seem to be intentional and malicious, but we must remember that reporters rarely read the books in question, or study the history behind events. Many of their false premises come from sheer ignorance. If one does not read any of Debord's books or do the minimal amount of research, one can then write as if the Situationist International had not been disbanded in

1972, and then take off on flights of fancy as to what they are up to in the present—possibly terrorism. Another popular tactic is the diversion. Perhaps starting from a truth or half-truth, the journalist takes a detour into speculation, most often entertaining and titillating, without notifying the reader that he has left the realm of fact. In reading *Considerations*, take note of the heavy use of the conditional tense in the news articles that Debord quotes at length. It seems that something great and portentous is being reported, but it is all air and innuendo. The use of anonymous sources allows reporters tremendous leeway in this direction. This technique is allied to the general trend in society whereby more and more people consider themselves to be artists. Journalists are no longer salaried hacks; they are also part-time novelists. And who are we to criticize if they sometimes get confused as to when they are writing fact or fiction?

Last but not least, there is the *ad hominem* or personal attack, which in the case of Guy Debord is taken to new heights. In these times, personality is much more enticing than ideas. And so someone like Debord will be placed on the psychiatrist's couch and his motivations dissected—he is not really interested in revolution, but rather personal power, influence, money, a comfortable life, what everyone else is interested in. His desire for privacy, or his disinterest in celebrity is actually a sign that he has something to hide, no doubt a dark and disturbing trait in his personality. Such psychologizing is no different from astrology, or talk of demon possession. And in the case of Debord, it serves two functions: entertainment, and the venting of intense, almost obsessive hatred of the man.

In the intervening years, this irrationality has only gotten worse, in the media and in the society it serves. Such illogic not only allows reporters to get away with murder, it also allows others greater leeway to commit murder, and get away with it. While those who manage the spectacle, or operate smoothly within it, are often able to plan ahead, to strategize success through a sequence of steps, they can also depend on the media and the public to fumble about in the darkness, unable to reason or see through the mysteries around them. (Of course, society's irrationality also infects those in power, who frequently miscalculate.)

Debord's book is an example of the spectacle-in-action, an indication of the new terrain it is occupying, and its adaptability. As Sun-tzu wrote, "So what enables...extraordinary accomplishments is foreknowledge. Foreknowledge cannot be gotten from ghosts and spirits, cannot be had by analogy, cannot be found out by calculation. It must be obtained from people, people who know the conditions of the enemy."

Robert Greene

Guy Debord

The most indulgent of all centuries, one that has general-ly found anything that was imposed upon it as most agreeable, has judged me with a great severity, and even with a sort of indignation. It has never hidden its intense revulsion when speaking about me, as well as anything that resembles me. But nevertheless, it has had to talk about me. It has done this, of course, in its own manner, which is inimitable: for our times do not resemble any other, and baseness is everywhere.

In all, whatever the subject matter, I believe I haven't read more than five or six true facts that have been reported about me; and never two together. And these same facts were almost always taken out of context and further distorted by several errors added on to them; and then, these facts were re-interpreted with much malevolence and foolishness. Everything else written about me is pure invention. These inventions, extraordinarily diverse but always having the same intentions, supply material for just as many new interpretations, often of a surprising irrationality—surprising because it should actually be quite simple for the inventor, who endlessly and arbitrarily makes things up about me, to create stories that are more or less believable, without too many apparent contradictions, while also coming to the conclusions he wants. Never have so many false witnesses surrounded a man so obscure.

Nothing, however, in more than 30 years of false ignorance and blatant lies, was so concentrated and so inept in its spectacular falseness as the reports that the French press on all sides resorted to in the aftermath of March 5, 1984, the day that Gérard Lebovici, my publisher and friend, was drawn into an ambush and assassinated in Paris.

Since I find myself, as much by nature as by the singular place I occupy in society and in contemporary history, very far removed from any kind of personal polemic, it would require something this unfortunate and despicable to draw me out of my habitual and disdainful silence, and to oblige me this time to "answer a fool according to his own folly, lest he be wise in his own conceit."

Since I am dealing with such a jumbled pile of

nonsense, I will repeat what others have said in a similarly disordered manner, showing what this systematic distortion of reality is and what it means. I would display too much honor to my subject were I to treat it in an orderly fashion. I want to show that it is unworthy of such a treatment.

This century does not like truth, generosity or greatness. Therefore it did not like Gérard Lebovici, who drew upon himself more than the usual amount of hateful envy through his freedom of thought and his culture. He therefore had many enemies, since "as long as the inverted world happens to be the real world" (Marx), the rarest of personal qualities will pass for the worst faults. Among so many enemies, those who had their particular reasons for getting rid of him could count on the abundance of others wanting to do the same, knowing that the forest can hide a tree. You don't have to actually pay people to make sure that they will bark with unmitigated joy when the man, whose mere existence makes them shamed, is finally killed. It is enough to have molded them and to know them, and they will do the rest. Thus, journalists, having completely identified themselves with the unknown assassins, immediately knocked each other over trying to supply the killers with reasonable motives and to attribute to the victim all sorts of flaws that in one way or another would amply justify his death. And among the reproaches, the one that has been thrown at him the most consistently and violently, is the only one that is true, namely that he made the unforgivable mistake of knowing me.

A few hours after the discovery of the crime, on March 7, *l'Agence France-Presse* released this surprising report: "The film producer Gérard Lebovici...Paris—At the time of the May 1968 Movement, he was one of the masterminds behind the Situationist International, alongside Guy Debord, his longtime friend whose complete film works he showed at the Studio Cujas in Paris, which Lebovici had just recently purchased. After May '68, Lebovici launched the publishing house Champ Libre which has produced more than 150 books tied to the May movement and also *L'Instinct de Mort* by Jacques Mesrine."[1] Unfortunately it is not true that, alongside me, Gérard Lebovici masterminded the Situationist International "at the time of the May 1968 Movement." That is quite a shame: he deserved such an honor. But I only met him three years later.

L'Agence France-Presse went into more detail in a report the following day, March 8: "M. Gérard

Lebovici, the film producer who Wednesday morning was found dead in a public parking lot on the Avenue Foch in Paris, with two bullets in the head, was also the chairman and managing director of the publishing house Champ Libre, which started off with a decided 'situationist' bent, as an associate of his pointed out. Lebovici's wife was the director of this publishing house. Champ Libre, which to this day has published 150 titles, had become well known for publishing the works of Guy Debord, the leader of the Situationist International, a current of thought with a decided libertarian bent, which played a very important role in the student and intellectual movement of May '68 in France." It is even more inaccurate to describe Champ Libre as a publishing house with a "situationist" bent, whether referring to its early years or to later on. Champ Libre has published in the following order works by Joseph Déjacque, Korsch, *Baltasar Gracian*, Boris Pilniak, *Clausewitz*, Cieszkowski, Fernando Pessoa, *Bakunin*, Ribemont-Dessaignes, Malévitch, Bruno Rizzi, Li T'ai Po, Satie, Souvarine, Jomini, Ciliga, Junius, Hegel, colonel Ardant du Picq, Groddeck, Omar Khayyam, Jens-August Schade, *Anacharsis Cloots*, Borkenau, Jorge Manrique, Richard Huelsenbeck, Sexby, *Orwell*, Marx, Vaugelas, General Napier, Gérald Brenan, Herman Melville, *Saint-Just*, and many others.

For those names in italics, it published their complete works. Unless everything of quality is generously referred to as "situationist," it would be hard to find anything situationist in the authors I have just taken the effort to cite.

Let us move on to the ridiculous application of the words "student and intellectual" to a movement that was so unmistakably proletarian and revolutionary. It must be said that the article's reference to this "current of thought with a decided libertarian bent, which played a very important role" in 1968 is not a historical reminder, but rather a recent discovery of *l'Agence France-Presse*. You will not find such an importance mentioned in any newspaper of the time, and in very few books that have appeared since. What a curious delay, in this day and age in which information flows so quickly! *l'Agence France-Presse* needed almost 16 years to be able to reveal such a scoop. But in fact, they knew this all along.

Each newspaper, owner of its own special source of confidential historical memories, continues the work of *l'Agence France-Presse*, adding its own little insignificant nuance. On March 9, *France-Soir*[2] divulged the following: "One of the most mysterious of men seems to possess the secret entrance to those clandestine anarchist circles that so fascinated Gérard Lebovici. That mystery man is filmmaker and writer Guy Debord, 54 years old, the éminence grise of Champ Libre, head of the 'situationists,' a movement with libertarian tendencies which was one of the detonators of the explosive events of May '68." "One of the detonators" implies that there are others that could be discovered. But on March 16, *Rivarol*[3] simplified the whole problem in an excellent manner by explaining, in one easy stroke, this particular "fascination" with the situationists, describing Lebovici as a "fanatic of the Situationist International, a political and revolutionary movement which was the source of the events of May '68." While on March 13, *L'Humanité*[4] talks about "an intellectual as mysterious as he is incongruous: Guy Debord, founder and then gravedigger of the Situationist International.... A strange character, this Debord. Author of ultra-leftist theories which had their hours of glory during May '68, he appeared to be able to obtain from the film producer Lebovici just about anything he asked for...."

Does this stalinist journalist reproach me more for having been among those who founded the Situationist International, or 15 years later, for being the main person responsible for its auto-dissolution? I believe that he is equally displeased by both. And maybe, from his point of view, he is not wrong: the two acts, each in their time, were equally revolutionary. But it is false to say that these theories "had their hours of glory during May '68." As I remember it, nobody mentioned such theories at the time; and this obscuring of the facts has obviously not stopped since then. It was an hour of glory for the workers of Paris. I am only "mysterious" for those who do not know how to read me, or for those who have only heard of me through the professors of lies who have so often hidden what I have actually written and what I have actually done. I don't understand what the journalist means by "incongruous." What is more incongruous than a stalinist in this day and age?

Besides a few brief references to the auto-dissolution of the Situationist International that, without explaining why, is usually presented as yet another shameful deed, the general tendency is to act as if the Situationist International exists today; and if we allow the times we live in to instruct us, this still living Situationist International would be even more frightening than in the days when people already were loath to admit its existence. On March 17, *Minute*[5], less embarrassed than those dissemblers who want to be thought of as being lightly on the left, dared to propose the following definitive definition: "But what then is situationism? What is its program? Briefly put, it is the following: 'Discredit the good. Compromise all bosses. Unsettle their beliefs. Deliver them up to general disdain. Make use of base and vile men. Disorganize all authority. Sow discord among the citizenry. Stir up the young against the old. Ridicule all traditions. Disrupt supply lines. Make people listen to lascivious music. Spread lewdness.'" In order to gauge the seriousness of this sort of theorizing, it must be noted that *Minute* does not try to hide the fact that it found these words in the book of a simple novelist who, while being a monarchist, is generally not credited with even the realism of a Balzac. It is naïve to claim to be able to explain, without any other research, events and historical ideas by means of formulaic phrases that originate from the fantasies of a novelist. Finally, I would like to point out that I cannot see how I could possibly be reproached for making people listen to lascivious music.

Each period uses a particular vocabulary to exorcise the demons that plague it. At the time when the situationists were an active force, they were rarely referred to or treated as terrorists, even though the idiotic concept of "intellectual terrorist" was purposely popularized in reference to them. But the Situationist International was dissolved in 1972, at a time when artificial terrorism had just begun, a terrorism which, henceforth, was to be so much in vogue for the governing of states and which, in the crusade to defeat it, has granted these same states their certificates of democracy. If the Situationist International still existed today, it would inevitably be called a terrorist group. And that is precisely why certain strategists, and the trumpeters who follow at their heels, would like to make believe that it still exists.

In this vein, on March 23 *Le Nouvel Observateur*[6] asked itself: "In the end, isn't King Lebovici no more than a man under the influence? Since knowing Debord, has he not drifted towards extremist organizations such as the Red Brigades or Direct Action, groups he could have financed because of his taste for scandal and provocation? The police did not find his name on the files of French Red Brigades—which have been thoroughly infiltrated and monitored—and in Rome they say that the anarcho-maoist-lenininsm of Champ Libre was 'light years away from the archeo-leninism' of the Brigades...." What they say in Rome is condemned by all those who still are able to think in this world. The Great Prostitute of spectacular terrorism[7] has recently and officially confessed that its special services, with the complicity of the useful elements of the Mafia and Vatican, have been consistently present in all of the bloody operations that have been conducted since 1969, under the command of Italy's parallel government, which has managed to shelter itself under the sensitive pseudonym of P.2. These confessions were not proof enough to make *Le Nouvel Observateur* decide to open up its files. And its naïve researchers even boast of having made inquiries in Rome. They could have saved themselves the trip if they had only read Champ Libre's catalog and learned right then and there that one cannot discern the slightest trace of leninism or maoism in its list.

On March 10, *Présent*[8] wrote: "The façade of being a prosperous show-business entrepreneur, of having reached the summit of success, also hid a more alarming activity: that of being the patron of the extreme left. After May '68, he established the publishing house Champ Libre, where he published thinkers and strategists of the terrorist and libertarian left. Among the house writers there was the enragé Guy Debord, head of the 'situationists,' the most nihilistic, the most destructive of all the anarcho-surrealist movements, probably the main promoter of subversion during May '68. Through this center of leftist propaganda, Lebovici's contacts extended to all the groups involved in international terrorism. He maintained contact in Germany with the Baader gang, as well as in Italy with the Red Brigades. In a general way, all of the dynamiters of bourgeois society, of Christian and Western civilization fascinated this Jew.... Subsidizing subversion—whether out of conviction or pleasure or hatred for the established order or worldly snobbery—has its risks."

The only proof, if it dared be said, that Gérard Lebovici subsidized subversion, and that his contacts "extended to all the groups involved in international terrorism," is that he knew me, "probably the main promoter of subversion during May '68." But equally true, the only proof that I myself ever had the slightest contact with this mythical "international terrorism"—whose ideas and methods are so obviously a stranger to and enemy of the profound subversion of which 1968 is truly an important example—is that I knew Gérard Lebovici.

I am to be counted "among the house writers." I have already cited several others. But I have never been the "éminence grise" of Champ Libre's many publications. I have never acted as its director, nor have I exercised any kind of function there. I have been so discreet as to not even step foot in their offices since 1971. From now on, I will go there whenever necessary.

The fact that Gérard Lebovici financed subversion—immediately accepted as self-evident and based on the scientific reasonings we have just seen—now allows these news sources to roll several specific actors of this protean subversion like dice, as if they were interchangeable illustrations of the truth revealed, and of course without being compelled to choose a single real example which would have the slightest pretense of being convincing. On March 13, *France-Soir* wrote: "Gérard Lebovici was, on the other hand, a very important provider of funds for certain ultra-leftist cliques, all under the sphere of influence of the 'situationist' movement that came out of May '68.... Why not imagine that this impresario-patron had suddenly desired to cut off or reduce the financial aid that he was giving them? In such a case, this decision would have been greeted by anger, even violence by those affected.... Certain followers of the situationist movement have been very close to terrorist groups like 'Direct Action,' which for a long time has maintained very close ties with 'Prima Linea,' the Italian organization that was the rival to the Red Brigades. This is the infamous 'Italian trail.' In this vein, some people have pointed out that Madame Lebovici-Floriana is the daughter of a dental surgeon from Turin."

There is not a single ultra-leftist clique that is

"under the sphere of influence of the situationist movement"—that's what would one think, and assume everyone would know, before taking into consideration the fact that the public has long since been conditioned to consume the society of the spectacle's specious reasonings. And knowing this about such cliques in the first place would most definitely have prevented Gérard Lebovici from ever funding them. But since such extreme-leftist situationist factions have been posited as fact, "why not imagine," in fact, that he one day desired to be rid of them? Such an audacious desire would of course have caused much anger, and there are people whom it is dangerous to make angry; indeed, the word violence is a little weak these days to describe such a swift and severe reaction—four bullets in the head for initiating an argument. With Gérard Lebovici the press would then have a very convenient guilty party, for if it is difficult to point a finger at "a sphere of influence," it is easy enough to designate its evil leader. It is a rather unrefined, not to mention anachronistic, accusation to suppose that some "followers" of this situationist movement could have become, 12 years later, "very close" to groups such as "Direct Action." And why not then to Captain Barril?[9] Let us mention in passing the bit of reasoning that would like to confirm "the Italian trail." There seems to be a new racism that wants to insinuate that all Italians must be seen as terrorists; or perhaps only all of its dental surgeons?

I do not know if the story of my life, which has been stirred by so many different adventures, but always in the same direction, would truly suffice (without any other kind of trial) to condemn someone who simply had the boldness to publish my books. But evidently, Gérard Lebovici had done more than that, and even when it comes to the question of publishing books, he has been unjustly accused of yet a more unacceptable perversity. The rumor, false like all the rest, has sometimes made the rounds that he had "secretly" handed over to me "the control of his publishing house," as *L'Humanité* had written on March 15. In the days after the assassination, this rumor was warmed up again by people who did not shrink from taking advantage of such a circumstance to repeat this falsehood, personally dear to them, to anyone who would listen.

It's at this point that a bit of buffoonery interrupts the drama as a kind of interlude and is used most opportunistically to clarify the whole affair according to the interests of the forces of repression. Four Champ Libre employees were fired in November 1974, four years after the publishing house had begun its activities.

These four were Messieurs Guégan, Guiomar, Le Saux and Sorin, all of whom have since continued their careers by working for different newspapers, most notably for the literary section of *Le Monde.*

Thus, on March 10 [1984] there appeared in *Le Monde*, under the name of Monsieur Sorin, the following: "I see before my eyes Lebovici as he appeared that Monday, November 4, 1974. Keaton mask-like face, raincoat à la Bogart, arriving for a meeting he had arranged at La Coupole. Right away he asked for the resignation of Guégan. Guégan refused. Going around the table, one by one we did the same thing, refusing to resign. A half-hour later, we walked away from Lebovici, leaving him Champ Libre, along with all the funding, the future projects, an image and a legend.... A representative of capital, attentive, enlightened—he had paid us very poorly, but had left well enough alone. We had proposed publishing writers he was not acquainted with: Celma, Burroughs, Delahaye, Dietzgen, etc. Guégan had put him in contact with Guy Debord and the members of the Situationist International.... We revealed to him our refusal to yield to his 'personal tastes.' For the first time, he addressed to us one of those letters which, among many others, figure prominently in his two volumes of letters published under the

name *Correspondance.* Moreover, by publishing this letter he broke the silence concerning our breakup; we had
decided, by mutual agreement, to refrain from 'any kind
of commentary concerning the reasons for [our] parting
of the ways.' In a few months he turned what was once
a place full of life into a museum.... In order to respond
to the rumors that pointed to 'the hand of Debord' in
this seizure of power at Champ Libre, he also published
a letter of Debord's to Jaime Semprun, the author of
Précis de récuperation [published by Champ Libre]. We
all thought that Debord's opinions, which [Guégan's
book] *Les Irréguliers* takes aim at, were the determining
factors in Lebovici's 'going into action' and his meta-
morphosis into a dialectician and revolutionary.
Debord's statements concerning his role as editor ('I
deserve credit for the publication of Cieszkowski or
Anacharsis Cloots') are inaccurate."

This short text calls for an analysis and a number
of refutations. First, M. Sorin hides the true and surprising motive for the conflict—the complete docu-
mentation (their letters and the response of the publisher) can be read in Volume I of *Correspondance* (published by Champ Libre). After several disagreements
whose details I do not know, these four "intellectual
workers," as they themselves like to be called, presented

Gérard Lebovici with a short-term ultimatum. They wanted to overcome the differences of opinion in the most direct way: namely, that "the control of production and the management of Champ Libre" be given over to a committee of six people, of which they held four of the positions. The publisher responded to this absurd putsch with a lengthy refutation of their allegations, and arranged for a meeting. During this meeting, he told them that since he refused their demands, he was waiting for their resignations. They replied "that they wouldn't even consider the question" of resigning. At that point the publisher made it clear that they were all immediately fired. What else could they expect?

"He paid very poorly, but left well enough alone." As it is well-known that Gérard Lebovici has never been accused by anyone of not being liberal or free with money, I suppose that if he paid them little, it is because he reckoned their services were not worth much. That he left well enough alone is contradicted by the fact that they themselves complained of his "personal tastes" and lack of generosity, his refusals and vetoes, his constant criticisms, the censorship that he finally imposed on their weak intellectual endeavors and their conciliatory, worldly practices. Their intention is to depict an uncultured financier, an inept "patron," who should have been delighted to have found such brilliant minds. If that had been the case, they would have then already owned Champ Libre, and someone would have had to have come from the outside to steal from them their own publishing house—for it is rather strange to imagine that a publisher would have to "seize power" at his own company. They are content to believe that this outsider is me, undoubtedly a better terrorist than they are. An unexpected conspiracy would have swept away another, one that already imagined itself having attained power; and this is what has left a permanently dubious cloud of conspiracy—against the entire world—around this publishing house.

I willingly believe that they proposed to the publisher certain authors that he did not know about. They mention these writers themselves: Celma, Burroughs, Delahaye, Dietzgen. One can see the significance of this. They brought his attention to the writers that they knew about; on the other hand, it is untrue that Guégan "had put him in contact with Guy Debord." I did not know M. Guégan.

As for breaking "the silence concerning our breakup," this silence is actually what M. Sorin calls having "decided by mutual agreement" to refrain from any kind of commentary. The four of them, for reasons that must have seemed desirable, had deposited a paper signed with their four names and soliciting the signatures of the two people in charge of Champ Libre. These two did not even respond to this (see *Correspondance, I*). The discreet surrender that they hoped for had even been presented in the style of a putsch manqué. And they thought, or wanted to think, undoubtedly "by mutual agreement," that I had been involved in some way or other in this affair. A little later I read Guégan's *Les Irréguliers*. It's a sorry thing, like everything that M. Guégan writes, but I swear that I could not discern in any way how it had "taken aim" at me. And even if I had figured out the connection to myself, how could that possibly be of any interest to me? I have been a more easily recognizable character in several dozen bad novels. And as for those novels sometimes constructed by newspapers, with their infinitely more considerable circulation, I have always been completely indifferent to them. As I have said, an extremely particular set of circumstances required me this time to respond.

M. Sorin ventures to qualify as inaccurate—in the name of his famous accuracy and his well-known competence—some statements of mine contained in a letter that he did not want or know how to understand through simple reading. My thesis was that a publisher must be held responsible for all that he decides to publish, that it is therefore he who must receive all the blame or all of the praise. And in that context, I cited the examples of Cieszkowski and Anarchisis Cloots in such a way that it was natural to deduce that those names figured precisely among the very few authors that I myself made Gérard Lebovici familiar with, without making that my career, and without boasting of it later in the press. He in turn made me familiar with some writers as well.

In 1971, when Champ Libre offered to republish my book from 1967, *La Société du Spectacle*, recently "masperized"[10] by the publisher Buchet, I went two or three times to Champ Libre's offices, located at the time on the rue des Beaux-Arts. On one occasion, I exchanged a few words with M. Le Saux. The style of Champ Libre at the time was to illustrate all of its covers, and I wanted nothing else for the cover of my book than a geographic map of the world, in its entirety. Subsequently M. Le Saux sent me some design plans in his own style, representing the planet. But I am not one of those who regard his designs as "marking an epoch," (that is what *Le Monde* of March 9 said of him), and so

21

his drawings did not please me. I myself then chose from a turn-of-the-century atlas a map whose colors represented the worldwide development of commercial relations, where it stood at that time and the course it was expected to run in the future. I caught glimpses of M. Guégan in these offices. I do not recall him saying anything. During these visits I spoke with the publisher. Afterwards, M. Guégan wrote me a letter concerning the visit of a particular individual, and I answered him. I do not know M. Sorin. After 1971, I was not to be seen in the several successive locations of Champ Libre's offices. It is Gérard Lebovici who did me the honor of coming to see me at my house.

These gentlemen now talk about their good old days, their past merits, of Champ Libre's obvious regression when their services had become unnecessary, as if history had proven them right, and as if everyone had seen in the last ten years what they are truly capable of. It is always the same logical procedure, that of the three-card monte player begging the question. Have they realized any of their ambitions, as authors or publishers? Not at all, they have had a run of bad luck. They ran the publishing house Sagittarius, and made it bankrupt within a few months. Now that certain of them write for *Le Monde*, by an unfortunate coincidence this newspaper is collapsing. *Le Monde*, according to what one hears, has finally lost the respect of its readers, something it has not deserved for the last 20 years, but at least had been able to keep up the illusion otherwise. Now it no longer has the means.

Starting off with the same sources, *Le Journal du Dimanche*[11] of March 11 obviously arrives at the same conclusions: "Lebovici wanted to push [Champs Libre] further to the left. The person behind this push, for Guégan and his friends, is Guy Debord, the invisible man, Debord, the fanatic of himself: 'His only goal and thought is for posterity,' says Guégan. 'His disappearance, it's a trick so that people will be reading him in 30 years. He wanted to do like Rimbaud, who left for Africa and never wrote another line. But for Rimbaud, it wasn't a trick.'" These projections of M. Guégan do not say anything about me, but at least they say something about him. He is certainly among those who have helped spread the idiotic rumor that I "disappeared" after 1968 or whenever, whether it was in order to make bombs, or merely imbeciles, talk. The simple truth, however, perhaps more painful for the amateurs or the barons of the present social spectacle, is that in all my life I have never appeared anywhere.

On March 15 [the magazine] *VSD*[12] took up again the same bit of nonsense: "Under the influence of Guy Debord, whose book he published, Gérard Lebovici becomes another man: on November 4, 1974 he fires Gérard Guégan, dissolves the entire Champ Libre team and sequesters himself with his guru in the two-roomed office decorated with the covers of the 12 issues of the Situationist International. From this point on, Gérard Lebovici thinks like Debord. Lebovici's correspondence with his authors, published by Champ Libre, is a perfect example of this." Was it necessary to become "another man" in order to fire Gérard Guégan? And why was it necessary to believe in my influence in order to explain such a petty affair, one that I had absolutely nothing to do with, and that I only learned about months later in Italy, where I was living at the time? I have said that I no longer visited the offices of Champ Libre, located then on the rue de la Montagne-Sainte-Geneviève, and so I cannot know if they were decorated with the covers of the S.I. The word "guru" has the smell of the sect about it, and I was alone; it smells of a doctrine that offers some kind of salvation, and I have always been the enemy of fixating any thought into an ideological system; perhaps it smells of the secret and the occult, and what I have thought has continuously been exposed to the light of day: not in the "American night" of the spectacle, where all cows are gray. They use the term "guru" precisely because it is the exact opposite of everything that I am. And they know that.

Lebovici, they say, "writes like Debord"; and others will go even further, deducing that it is me who writes and that the other, "a man under the influence" if ever there was one, only had to sign his name without discussion. They know well enough, but do not tell the reader, that hundreds of individuals have written like me, taking up the style, the tone that I have used. They were, however, more often libertarian spirits than conformists or servants of a tyrant. If certain people have so much enjoyed my style, it is because of the examples of my life. They mention Gérard Lebovici with an air of astonishment, because he did this openly, while others have done it more secretly. According to definitions that would prove most convenient to certain people, a publisher should not know how to write, let alone read. We can recognize there the pretension of the fired employee, who assumed without question that he was indispensable. We have since been able to read Gérard Lebovici's manuscript notes, found after his murder, which map out his unfinished book, *Tout sur le personnage*[13]. We can thus see the truth and the great feel for dialectics that characterizes his theoretical reflections, at a time when sidewalk-vending thinkers are so esteemed for reinventing lukewarm water. But it really was with the letter of insults that he first showed himself as a writer. The letter of insults is a kind of literary genre which has occupied an important position in our century, and not without reason. I believe that no one would doubt that I myself have learned a lot in this area from the surrealists, and especially from Arthur Cravan. The only difficulty of the letter of insults is not the style, but rather having the confidence that you yourself are in the right at that moment, and that the letters are aimed at precisely the right people. They must never be unfair.

Other rash denunciations have come from the film milieu. On March 10, *France-Soir* summed them up in the following way: "Among people in the film world—most of whom were not aware of Gérard Lebovici's activities as a fringe publisher and patron of the writer and filmmaker Guy Debord, head of the situationists, sympathizer with the terrorist 'Baader' gang and the 'Red Brigades'—the question is asked more and more what could have been the motive for such an assassination?" Thus those who had worked with Gérard Lebovici in film, claimed that they did not know he was a publisher, and even claimed they did not know he had produced several of my films; such people have *ipso facto* helped contribute to the image of him as a man who lived a double life, a dissembler. He would have been leading such a life, using techniques that truly would have been those of a secret agent, had these people not been deliberately lying. But they have been lying; and under what "influence?" Although many journalists, who are no less uncultured than those in cinema, have all been quick to mention Champ Libre, the scandalous Studio Cujas, as well as the titles of almost all of my films since 1952—and with such a lack of affection, one might add—some people in the film business, in this scandalmongering village, have pathetically maintained they know nothing about all of this, and in short know nothing about a man who had made several of them rich and successful. We can see how this assassination has shown that the contempt the victim felt for this milieu for a long time is more than justified.

At the release of my last film in 1981, numerous ads in the film and non-film press had featured the catch-phrase "Gérard Lebovici presents," and it was the first time that such words had been used by this producer. This is a curious lapse on the part of a secret agent who would otherwise so easily hide his double life. This catch-phrase did not go unnoticed by those in the profession; it even made some of them jealous. In the same circles, the tactless director Alain Resnais was made fun of for taking up the same phrase, "Gérard Lebovici presents," for his last film, *L'Amour à mort*, the filming of which did not even commence until some days after the assassination. To claim to have a film presented by a dead man, that is the most original thing the filmmaker Resnais has done since *Hiroshima, mon amour*. He could have also had the film presented by Guillaume Apollinaire, or by Heraclitus. The method has a promising future; but not perhaps the inventor. Pioneers are not always universally misunderstood, but in being the first to do something, they do expose themselves to the dangerous consequences, or a gob of spit in the face.

It must be said that what we find here is a law firmly established in the French film world. Rather than make of me a kind of vague legend, as do leftists or thinkers who claim to explain this society, they question with much sincerity my very existence. They firmly believe that they do not know anything about me. And it is for a very good reason. If I had existed, then many of these film auteurs would have lost a certain part of their reputation as innovators; and some would have completely lost it.

And so this is why (although for some, other necessities are certainly involved) all of these malicious snitches, pretending to ask themselves "more and more what could have been the motive for such an assassination," hurried to the police to help direct the investigations with their cock-and-bull stories.

On March 15, the same *VSD*, whose wealth of information we have already been able to appreciate, summed up my life and work in the following way: "Guy Debord summed up his thinking in the work *La Société Spectacle*, a manifesto in which he explains that the world is nothing more than an illusion staged and directed by the media, that the proletariat must wake up, seize power and establish self-management. Guy Debord loves scandal: avant-garde filmmaker, he manufactured a film entitled *Hurlements en faveur de Sade* that is without images and with a soundtrack interrupted by long silences. He also loves to provoke: he hates, in a jumbled manner, stalinists, capitalists, journalists, and even leftists. He has fallen out with all of his friends, one after the other." This new title ascribed to my book shows, beyond a doubt, their desire to confuse it with a recent imitation by a certain Schwartzenberg, *L'État-spectacle*, or with the concept, less annoyingly Debordian, that many commentators for some years have delicately nuanced, when they prefer to speak of the "society of spectacle." It is not true that I have had a falling out with all of my friends, one after the other. My friends are those with whom I have not had a falling out. I am even less accustomed to having friends killed, although that seems to be the implication. Their enumeration of what I "hate" only proves more clearly my lucidity and my good taste.

It is because of all of this, and not only because of the film that I "manufactured" in 1952, that an article in *France-Soir* that appeared on March 8 (the same day in which the news of the assassination became public) called me "an eccentric writer and filmmaker." For anybody else, some originality would have been recognized. Since the time of my first film, certain filmmakers have taken 20 or 30 years to come closer to a cinema without images: they have been praised for their patience. To give another amusing example—the painter Yves Klein, whom I knew at the time of *Hurlements* and who attended the first, very tumultuous showing of this film, was dazzled by a convincing 24 minute-sequence of darkness, and must have derived from that, some years later, his "monochrome" paintings which—enveloped in a bit of zen mysticism during his famous "blue period"—made many an expert cry genius. Some still call him that. When it comes to painting, it is not I who could possibly obscure the glory of Yves Klein. That is, rather, what Malévitch had done 40 years before, and which had been temporarily forgotten by these same experts.

Gérard Lebovici, whom this issue of *France-Soir* describes as "a genius in business, the most important agent-producer in French cinema," was in an excellent position to know that I had accomplished in film what nobody else had even tried to do, and what nobody even knew how to imitate with any kind of talent. I have succeeded in universally displeasing, and in a way that is always new.

A lot of ink has been spilt over the fact that Gérard Lebovici had purchased a space in the Latin Quarter in order to show only my films there. Such a "gift" has been viewed as extravagant. If, according to such journalists, a filmmaker should not accept this kind of gift from a friend, it must be asked what concept of friendship can these poor men have? And what gifts can be given to them, from their friends, if they have any?

They say that this screening room proved to be very expensive, since audiences were small. Business people of today have lost all sense of proportion. Those of the 19th century had not reached such extremes. They no doubt found the writings of Mallarmé scandalous, but for other reasons. They would not have rebuked him in such a tone for the non-profitable aspect of his works. Gérard Lebovici was not at all interested in money. Me neither, as everyone knows; and this is only one of numerous points in which we were alike. His character was such that he was driven to respond violently to abnormal situations which others would accommodate themselves to, or maybe would not even feel as abnormal. The unthinkable way in which these publications have commented on his assassination have led me to the decision that none of my films will be shown ever again in France. This absence will be a more than just homage.

The press wonders with one voice, with a naïve anger, what methods, what sorcery could I have used to influence Gérard Lebovici to such a point, to bewitch him, as they say? "Guy Debord, in the life of Lebovici, plays the part of darkness. 'The Devil.' A third-rate Mephistopheles in a real tragedy: that of the bewitchment of a man. Behind the most hidden face of Gérard Lebovici, there is always Guy Debord. It is because of him that Lebovici led a double life and, as soon as he left his C.E.O. offices on the rue Keppler, he changed

himself verbally into a super-leftist, admirer and publisher of Mesrine.... What evil spell ties the laughable
ex-May 68er to the king of Parisian film?" (*Le Journal
du Dimanche,* March 11).

"And so this man was the friend, the patron, the
financier, the accomplice of the scum of the revolutionaries from the bazaar of May 1968? He was the admirer of this man who is the dregs of non-thought, of this
pitiful incarnation of the 'spirit that negates?' So this
crafty and relentless businessman who cornered the
market on the most bankable stars and made the film
world tremble to such a point that a suit was brought
against him for his monopolistic schemings, this man
had allowed himself to be impressed, to the point of
being fascinated, by a pale little scribbler, a provincial
guru who was lifted into the clouds for eight days [dur-
ing May '68] by a handful of mindless slobs because he
covered worthless pages with his wild and indecipher-
able ramblings and meters of film with his vague and
fuzzy images?" (*Minute,* March 17).

"In 1971, the myth, perhaps the whiff of danger,
enters into the life of Gérard Lebovici, via Guy
Debord.... What actually happens between Debord and
Lebovici? Difficult to determine. Seduction? Lebovici,

who spent his life reassuring and encouraging his actors, was he in turn reassured by Guy Debord? One thing is certain: between the impresario-publisher and the 'Pope' who as early as 1957 proclaimed, 'Our ambitions are clearly megalomaniacal, but not measurable, according to the reigning criterion of success,' the 'Pope' who later wanted to make himself 'even more inaccessible, even more clandestine,' between these two men something clicked. It is tempting to explain it by the old magical attraction of a utopia.... On the one side, the pursuit of activities that are typical of an impresario and producer. On the other side, the marginality, a hidden master whom Lebovici still spent several days with near Nîmes, the week before his death." (*Le Point*[14], March 19).

"He let himself be very quickly seduced by the ideas of this ephemeral and self-dissolved movement. He who was at the financial heart of French cinema paradoxically promoted the 'non-cinema' of a Guy Debord who proclaimed as long ago as 1959: 'There are some people these days who have convinced themselves that they are authors of films like one used to be of novels. Their backwardness compared to novelists is that they are unaware of the decay and the impoverishment of all individual expression in our times, unaware of the end of the arts of passivity.' It is also Debord who wrote that same year: 'In reality one never contests the existence of an organization without contesting all of the forms of language that belong to this organization.' More than ten years later, Gérard Lebovici met Guy Debord. And the producer—all the while diversifying his film activities and up to the present undoubtedly becoming irreplaceable—developed a passion for the man who for many years spoke of 'the withering away of art' and who then returned to obscurity, at the end of the 1970s, telling the world: 'For me there will never be a turning back nor a reconciliation. Prudence and moderation will never come.'" (*Le Quotidien de Paris*[15], March 15).

"A revolutionary publishing house. It is called Champ Libre, and very quickly it becomes the meeting place for situationists—those heirs of dadaism and lettrism who, as early as the 1950s, had opened up the radical critique of capitalism and communism and to whom are due the great ideas and the better slogans of May '68. Lebo discovers there a world that impassions him, and one day there's the meeting—for him revelatory—with a man, Guy Debord, 'Pope' of the situationists, and his book *La Société du Spectacle*. What is it about Debord that can fascinate to such an extreme a man like Lebo? Does he see in him the theoretician of the spectacle-society, the man who in fact demolishes the media, warns against the commodified image, in other words, undermines from top to bottom what happens to be, in theory, the universe of Gérard Lebovici, impresario and producer? In any case, under the growing influence of Debord, Lebovici is transformed, splits into two, undoing in the dark of night the values that he supports during the day. And it is apparently without any problem that he takes on this dual role as man of the spectacle and theoretician of the anti-spectacle." (*Le Nouvel Observateur*, March 23).

"In 1971, a man presents himself to Gérard Lebovici as being a representative of Guy Debord; Lebovici, who at the time is the powerful owner of Artmedia, is going to become passionately interested in the founder of the Situationist International. He will produce his films and buy a small cinema which will become a kind of 'living museum' dedicated to the film works of Debord: *Hurlements en faveur de Sade* (1952), *La Société du Spectacle* (1973), and his last film *In girum imus nocte et consumimur igni* (1978). These films—which in fact are not films but rather a mass of collages, détournements of images, photos, voice-overs reciting text that is clever and of course without any concessions towards what Debord calls the 'Society of the

Spectacle'—are going to strangely seduce the man who has in his agency the biggest names in French cinema. How to explain then that Gérard Lebovici lets himself be bewitched (even so far as to 'support' him) by the man who writes in 1959, 'The only interesting endeavor is the liberation of everyday life, not only within the perspective of history, but for us now, immediately. This occurs through the withering away of alienated forms of communication. The cinema is to be destroyed as well...' Debord, because of his intransigence, his 'global critique of the idea of happiness,' his 'bringing into action a systematic doubt regarding all the diversions and labors of a society,' his disdain for every writer, filmmaker, journalist, artist (and in particular those who are said to be avant-garde), his hatred of communists, leftists or any political figure, has found himself very quickly isolated from one and all and forced to 'disappear.'" (*Le Quotidien de Paris*, March 14).

I do not know why I am called "a third-rate Mephistopheles" by people who are incapable of figuring out that they have been serving a third-rate society and have received in return third-rate rewards, food and housing. Or is it perhaps precisely because of that that they say such things? That the 1968 movement had been fundamentally insignificant, that is exactly what is contradicted by their wrath, still so intense 16 years later. And, personally, it is known that I have been the least insignificant of the leaders from those days, and the one that has been the least recuperated since then. "The spirit that negates" has certainly been pitiful in this era. One doesn't choose his era, although one can transform it. The "dregs of non-thought"—and this can no longer be disguised—are those who have ceaselessly led this world, from error into stupidity, up to the point where we now see it. It is very false to say that I was "lifted into the clouds for eight days by a handful of mindless slobs," since I know very well that they did not do that for even two days, not even one day. "Provincial guru" is amusing. It is the custom of newspapers to occasionally question whether I was ever a Parisian— from the day I was born to the moment that the city had changed so much that it was no longer worth living in, when I already was more than 40 years old. Perhaps it is an allusion to the fact that I live part of the year in provincial Arles? That little town of today was also once the provisional capital of the Empire of decadence. "Pope" is a derogatory word that has been systematical- ly applied to André Breton, which is already a ridiculous slander in this case, even if Breton toyed a little bit with charisma and hierarchical authority, and did that for more than 40 years, which was really far too long. It would certainly be tempting to explain many things by "the old magical attraction of a utopia," but for many it is more distressing to have to explain such things through the force of a real critique of the real world. "A hidden master," whether he lives near Nîmes or in the château de Montségur, brings to mind the world of sects, the "hidden Ayatollah," the Old Man of the Mountain and his ever-ready band of Assassins, or perhaps the mysterious Knights Templar as well. A self-dissolved movement which lasted for fifteen years (1957-1972), and which left so many marks cannot be called "ephemeral." Are the situationists hated so much because they are wrong or because they are right? One does not hate so much those who are wrong. Otherwise, how would we find political leaders to re-elect? Did I "return to obscurity at the end of the 1970s", or rather at the beginning? Would it not be fairer to recognize that I have never left it? I have said it, and I will repeat it in passing: the situationists have never had meetings at Champ Libre. To say that I will obviously always remain faithful to my choice of rejecting this society, its celebrities, and its spectacle of lies, and thus also to the clandestine life that I have been continuously thrown back into for several decades, that is what they want to confuse with political clandestine activity, and that is now even purposefully confused with an "anti-democratic terrorism," to quote an expression that is used to sell to the Basques a democracy where the votes of the generals are counted separately. I have known at times, in my youth, depending on the period but especially depending on the country, some short periods of true clandestine activity. This is obviously totally different from a simple and easy clandestineness in relation to the miserable pomp of the spectacle. It is even more stupid to write like [the newspaper] *Le Quotidien de Paris* that my extremism, which has of course made me many enemies, has isolated me and "forced me to disappear." I have never, in this sense, disappeared. What are they imagining? If I would have had two or four times as many ordinary individuals as enemies, I would have ignored them just the same, and I certainly would not disappear before my time because of them. Until now, and this is totally forgotten, it is Gérard Lebovici who has been made to disappear.

The most remarkable of all these astounding articles is undoubtedly the one signed by a Monsieur Boggio in the March 15 *Le Monde*. I beg you to pay particular attention to it: "If you were to believe certain people, Gérard Lebovici in some way might have provoked the murder. 'If someone had to die in the film world,' confided a close friend who, like most of the people we interviewed, was anxious to remain anonymous, 'it would be him....' Thus, the fact that this energetic man, so active in the extroverted, self-promoting film world, allowed himself to come under the influence of Guy Debord, the loner, discreet to the point of being obsessional, was seen still yesterday as the sign of an inevitably fatal weakness. According to ten, twenty testimonial statements, Gérard Lebovici 'was going down a slope' that was gradually distancing him from the norm that is socially acceptable for his professional milieu, all because of an intellectual and psychological wandering led (they are sure of this) by Debord, the 'guru.' 'Too many provocations, too many public insults; all of this had to finish badly,' further explained a writer, who also wished to remain anonymous.... 'The idea was nevertheless seductive,' explained one of those who already dreams of writing the novel about Lebovici's death, 'namely that a publisher known for his taste for provocation, was killed for maybe having regained control of the situation, for having refused, just this once, what one was sure he would accept.'"

The writer (and his sources) wanted to show that the truly criminal conduct was not the murder of Gérard Lebovici, but rather the act of having led him— by different influences that are inexplicable although accepted as fact—to the point of "gradually distancing him from the norm that is socially acceptable for his professional milieu." And Monsieur Boggio became so carried away in this reasoning that he thoughtlessly used a very audacious phrase which gives the impression that he knew more than he let on, perhaps attributing this execution to the professional milieu of film—although in this instance he approves of their having recourse to a kind of death sentence for exceptional reasons, and pronounced by a private, or semi-private authority. Maybe Monsieur Boggio believes that as today's cinema is a work of imagination operating almost always within the perspective of the dominant organization of daily life, that, in return, this milieu has been delegated a kind of authority which permits it to sometimes imagine itself as a sort of State which by itself carries out capital and corporal punishments upon individuals who have too visibly distanced themselves "from the norm that is socially acceptable for [their] professional milieu?" Nevertheless, even though he believes this, he seems to be in a hurry to denounce other people. It is known that there exists, and not only in Russia or Chile, a number of journalists/policemen. At an hour when all the powers of State are not separating, but rather uniting—refuting in the process the theory of Montesquieu, while ensuring control of the State—we see the para-judicial power of the press unconcerned by the little trivialities whose observance was once required by the legal and judicial system. There are only anonymous and unknown witnesses, "ten, twenty testimonial statements"—but why not 50, 200 or more?—like this "writer who also wished to remain anonymous." (Is it a pornographic writer, or simply an author of detective novels? In fact, he is ashamed and prudent for some reason.) Is this the same person who "already dreams of writing the novel about Lebovici's death?" But will he dare to, even under a pseudonym? We shall see. This anonymous mass—anonymous except for Monsieur Boggio, who in signing his name to the article takes responsibility for confirming the existence of all these witnesses—comes to the conclusion ("they are sure of this") that the one responsible is Debord; that it is "an inevitably fatal weakness" to know me; in the same way, by the authority of a novel that is not yet written, they throw out to the public the hypothesis that Gérard Lebovici had been "killed for having regained control of the situation, for having refused, just this once, what one was sure he would accept." And who else in the world could be certain that he would accept everything that might be useful to ask of him, if not me?

It seems difficult to understand why recourse to

sorcery and bewitchment would be required to explain a very natural reality: a publisher is interested in someone who writes like myself, simply because he has read me. If it were only a matter of my book, it could advantageously replace a thousand others. Almost 20 years ago, I designated in its totality a very important phase of capitalism, an entire epoch, with a name that will stay with it. And, if additional explanations are necessary, all those who have had the opportunity to spend time with me will say that it is rather interesting, and sometimes pleasant, to know me personally. Finally, the mere fact that I have not at all wanted to be approached by the dreary celebrities of the day would give me, if there were such a need, a sufficient prestige around those who have the unfortunate obligation of having to be around them.

But like the proletariat, I am supposed to not exist in this world. Right away that would mean that Gérard Lebovici maintained dangerous dealings with ghosts. The retreat and decline of rational thought, so evident and so deliberately sought after in the spectacle, makes it so that any practice that takes place outside the official magic organized by the State—and the omnipresent mirror of the world where everything is presented backwards—is labeled black magic, the gurus' rallying of dark forces, voodoo, on and on. To say that two plus two equals four is in the process of becoming a revolutionary act. In France does one dare think of complicating matters by looking for the middle of the summer day at two o'clock? Terrorism! It is the sun that must be mistaken, and the government that is right.

In the end, they ascribe to me the role of a demiurge, all the more surprising since, in theory, I should not even exist. As a demiurge, I could do anything I wished: I could bewitch at will, and always with the active but inexplicable assumption that the other was less than a beast, an object. Of course, the truth is totally the opposite. Gérard Lebovici knew how to charm me in a way that very few people were able to do. That must be added to the list of his merits, not my crimes.

In this monotonous and repetitive unleashing of rage, the March 17 *Minute* reaches a level of true originality. Claiming that I have long been a Russian agent, exactly as they were once saying of Bakunin, they conclude that thanks to gold from Moscow which came to me in boxes, it is I, in fact, who supplied Gérard Lebovici with his highly suspicious wealth. This would indeed be my finest achievement.

This press campaign had barely been set in motion

before numerous journalists attempted to get an interview with me, ringing at my door or even telephoning me directly, despite the fact that my telephone numbers are always unlisted. They were all turned away by my friends. Dozens of photographers, in groups or individually, and even some cameramen, stationed themselves in front of my windows for several weeks, waiting to get a picture of me on the sly. It is comforting to note that all the time spent by these incompetents came to nothing, with only one exception—after months of trying, someone managed to get a blurry, and not very interesting silhouette taken through a telephoto lens by infiltrating the house next door. The photograph, coupled with some hateful commentary, was then published by *Paris-Match*. The journalists of today are so accustomed to the public's submission—even their complete delight—when faced with the press' voracious need for information (of which journalists are apparently the great priests, but in fact the hired help) that I truly believe that much of the press deems guilty the person who would claim to not have to explain himself before their authority. But for me, I have always found it a crime to speak with journalists or to appear on television, in other words, to collaborate in the slightest way with the great enterprise of the falsification of reality that is lead by the mass media. It is quite normal for me to think so, and consequently to act this way, since I published the theory on this a long time ago. The press gladly believes that all those who have access to this sort of celebrity of the moment want it, and indeed want it as often as possible. But I have nothing to sell. Discretion is not viewed well in these times. An article in the March 23 *Le Nouvel Observateur* provides a revealing demonstration of this: "'In my long career, I have never seen as strange and mysterious an affair as this one,' said an important police commander.... And he concluded, in a pensive tone: 'What do you expect— by living in secrecy, one dies in darkness.'" In this statement emerges a new sociological law which actually makes one pensive. This "important police commander" has just supplied a brilliant contribution to the theory of the spectacle. He introduces the definition of a new criminal offense. He who does not, of his own free will, make himself as visible as possible in the spectacle, lives in fact in secrecy, since all current communication in society passes through this mediation. He who lives in secrecy is a clandestine person. A clandestine person will be more and more likely to be considered a terrorist. In any case, a clandestine person is not able to frequent honorable people; and one would not therefore be terribly astonished if such person met a violent and mysterious death.

This theme of a clandestine existence, or even of simple disappearance, is tangibly supported by the absence of any recent photos of myself. The March 11 *Le Journal du Dimanche* says: "If you did not stand upon the barricades in May '68, you probably are not familiar with Guy Debord. The only thing you must know is that for the last ten years, this 'situationist' author has decided to 'disappear' in order to better stir the imagination of others. An almost complete disappearance: no residence, no photos (the last one is from 1959), no contacts beyond a very small circle of the faithful. The most faithful of all was Gérard Lebovici."

Paradoxically, in this clandestine period the press has published half a dozen photos of me, all of which were found in situationist publications. And I know that there exist many others. They insist upon the great age of these photographs, while they themselves are doing everything they can to make it all worse. The March 15 *VSD* featured a photo published in the 1967 edition of *La Société du Spectacle.* and described it in the following way: "Dating from 1959, one of the rare photos of Guy Debord, the situationist philosopher who inspired the anarchistic ideas of Gérard Lebovici." Only their lack of education and culture has prevented them from finding a rather recent photo of me, extracted with many others from my films and printed in my *Œuvres cinématographiques complètes,* published by Champ Libre. Described as "Debord at 45," it therefore dates from 1977. Because of the press' inability to find such things, we thus have their furious efforts (and their almost total failure) to capture a photo of me in 1984. In order to put an end to this insipid legend according to which I would like to hide myself from whomever, I am having a very recent photo of myself published in this book.

The *Journal du Dimanche* of March 11, using its favorite source—the same person who, in 1974, brought to light the entire epic of the heroes who embarked on the conquest of the publishing house Champ Libre—revealed the essence of the whole fascinating problem regarding the evolution of my disappearance: "However, the man with the briefcase wants to speak in the name of the most absolute of all revolutionaries: the founding father of the Situationist International (mini-grouplet with its bombastic-sounding name), which in its journal of the same name rejects all those who claim to think about and understand politics, including the leftists who they find too fond of state control. The man in the suit comes to speak in Debord's name because the latter is from now on in hiding. The last photo that we have of him shows a young man with short hair, wearing steel-rimmed glasses, looking like the double of the actor-director Roger Planchon." This implied reproach seems quite unfortunate for Roger Planchon. Always anxious for scrupulous adherence to the historic truth, I cannot help clearing this matter up, even if it leads me to burden another man with a heavy responsibility (it is known that certain schools of criminology or psychiatry have placed a very weighty importance on the study of head shapes or facial expressions). I am actually the exact double of the actor Philippe Noiret, when we were both young.

It is the March 18 *Le Journal du Dimanche* which draws up the most complete picture of my daily life, although from the point of view of a kind of systematic delirium. As happens so often in this text, it will be necessary for me to quote at length, for such things cannot be summarized, just as no one could invent them in quite the same way. "'He's a bloody strange one,' grumbled the police superintendent Jacques Genthial (this was before his dismissal from the Crime Unit) who after two hours of examination accompanied home Guy Debord, the guru, the damned soul in control of Gérard Lebovici, the producer who was assassinated in the parking structure on the Avenue Foch. The leftist 'Pope of situationism,' and quite a mysterious character, was in fact questioned at the quai des Orfèvres [police headquarters] as part of the difficult investigation into a strange murder."

But the tone rises quickly, going from a personal impression arbitrarily attributed to police superintendent Genthial, to an almost general conviction, ascribed to different police departments, based on files and observations that are completely imaginary: "And for many police officers, whether they belong to the Crime Unit, to the D.S.T.[16], or to General Intelligence[17], the most important trail leads to Guy Debord's entourage. In any event, they are convinced for the time being that Gérard Lebovici's death is somehow directly linked to what are described as the very suspicious 'contacts' of Debord. The least one can say is that, true to the legend he has created, Guy Debord did not appear to be very talkative: 'He did not understand. He did not know of any enemies of Lebovici. Could it be a matter of a regrettable mistake? In each instance, he does not know anybody, not Mesrine nor any terrorists.' On the other hand, the various police services know Guy Debord very well. And if he is a mystery among his own entourage, the Pope of the 'situationists' is not at all one for the men of the D.S.T. or those in General

Information. You be the judge!"

They make things up from beginning to end, but they do not make up just anything, or for no reason. They ascribe to me words that are ridiculous and indecent ("Could it be a matter of a regrettable mistake?"), words which are obviously a bad parody of the style of a Mafia capo. Objective in this particular instance, the March 13 *Libération*[18] wrote in a more sober manner: "Moreover, according to police sources, the questioning this weekend of Guy Debord, one of the big name situationists, revealed nothing." But, as this *Journal du Dimanche* article says, "you be the judge" of what follows, and you are going to have a laugh.

"Starting in 1968, Guy Debord begins to attract the attention of the General Intelligence section of the Paris Police Department. Very fond of revolutionary ideas, he participates in the student movements of the time. He is seen in meetings, observed at the front line of demonstrators. May '68 passes, Guy Debord continues on with his passion: the cinema. Lebovici, whom he meets a little later, will be his patron. In the meantime, Debord gets married. In 1970 he marries a beautiful Chinese woman from Shanghai, Alice Ho. Alice's mother, a restaurateur, had had a second marriage to a

German, who was a deserter from the Reich army, Wolf Becker. Alice Ho, from then on, was called Becker-Ho. The Becker-Ho family settles down in Paris. A few hundred meters from the Cluny museum. Mme. Becker-Ho buys a Chinese restaurant. At this time the D.S.T. is already keeping an eye on the restaurant, where it is thought that friends and agents of Communist China like to eat and hang out." If the General Information department managed to take an interest in me, 1968 seems to me a rather late date. I was not converted by the events of May '68. I have been a bandit longer than that. The cinema has not been my passion, and not even the anti-cinema. "What we saw him leave behind, without pain, was not the object of his love," as Bossuet would say. Here, I have the pleasure of calling attention to a true word, the only one perhaps in the article: Alice is indeed beautiful. But in my case nothing could happen without some clandestine ulterior motive. We fall immediately upon the daughter of Fu Manchu, the secret societies of Old China, the agents of bureaucratic China, the hellish gambling dens of old Macao. When I am not seeking to wrap myself in mystery, which happens all the time, I would be exploiting at the very least the charms of my wife or my lovers, since they claim that "in 1972, Guy Debord launches his wife into a film career. Several specialized magazines are interested in her. She acts in some shorts directed by her husband but financed by Lebovici." There is no point in commenting on what "specialized magazines" might mean in this instance. Besides, to use stars has not been a feature of my film style.

"That same year the men of the D.S.T. find themselves more and more interested in Debord. To them, there is no doubt that the 'Pope'—that is how he is described—is engaged in suspicious activities. But it would seem that some political figures—on the left as well as on the right—intervened and managed to have the dossier on Debord buried and forgotten." That same year is 1972. That starting from that time on, the D.S.T. was "more and more" interested in me, yet in the intervening 12 years since has found nothing, with anyone else one would reach the conclusion (in less time than that) that, after all, perhaps this person had been mistakenly suspected of acting on behalf of a foreign power, or of a more vague "international terrorism." But in my case "it would seem" that some political figures "on the left as well as on the right" had wanted to protect me. It is necessary to say on the left and right since so many political nuances have followed one another in power. It is well known that I have nothing to do with political figures and that, on the right or the left, I consider them all to be cut from the same cloth. Still, it is rather strange, not so much that these politicians have unanimously confirmed my judgment that they are all the same, but rather that they have thus thanked me for this with such humble modesty. It is, in fact, incredible. Almost as much as these Kremlin bosses whom I am supposed to have swindled so recklessly.

"In the same period, M. and Mme. Debord apparently 'take in and shelter' the daughter of a very powerful politician, which sets the agents of General Information on edge, since the daughter of this important person talks way too much." I have never known in any period of my life the daughter of a politician deemed "very powerful," nor slightly powerful, nor the daughter of one who still hoped to become powerful. But this perspicacious *Journal du Dimanche* knows for a fact that if I had known such a daughter, I would have taken advantage of her alleged blabberings, either to sell them to the Russians, or perhaps to shake down her unfortunate family.

"Just outside the Debord property in Bellevue-la-Montagne (Haute Savoie), where from June to September the married couple go to relax, that is where the General Information agents hide and photograph the weekend 'guests.' Debord remains as mysterious as ever. You cannot meet up with him without using a code; the shutters on the property remain shut except for the blinds in the kitchen." Here I am going to make a confounding revelation. If in summer a lot of the blinds of my house remain shut, it is an effective defense against flies. I am referring to the two-winged insect of the family Muscidae, and not to bothersome journalists or other police secret agents who would like to see themselves, figuratively, as flies on the wall. Also, what does the above-mentioned code tell us? It could prove useful to other busybodies. Moreover, these journalists are as ignorant of geography as they are of history. Bellevue-la-Montagne is not in Haute Savoie, but in Auvergne.

"He travels under a false name in Italy and Germany. But the General Information agents do not leave him any breathing space, following him wherever he goes. When Guy Debord moves into a luxurious apartment a few yards away from the church Saint-Nicolas-des-Champs, the General Information agents station themselves nearby and keep a watch on him through binoculars. When he leaves Paris and goes to live in Arles, where he resides at this moment, the General Information agents are once more hot on his heels. His telephone cannot be tapped because he does not have one. But they are still able to follow his every move. It is known that the 'Pope' of the situationists loves good food, pretty girls and the good life. But it is also known that he is in contact with Italian and German intellectuals who are themselves very close to revolutionary groups: the Baader gang or the Red Brigades." It is easy to imagine that I travel under a false name, especially in Italy and Germany, countries famous for their terrorists. That means that, for good reason, I use false identity papers. But these men who do not leave me "any breathing space" cannot name one of these false names to their colleagues in the press. Maybe the agents are simply having a joke at the journalists' expense. But one outcome of their investigation is more indisputable. They have proof that I like pretty girls and good food. Is that not a very widespread inclination? Not so much anymore it seems. Today, the simplest things always seem to be linked to a critique of society. It is true that I have not often felt inclined to experiment with "nouvelle cuisine," where some green pepper attempts to cover the taste of livestock that has been raised on chemicals, nor have I felt inclined to test out the ladies with fake voices who in laughably similar terms extol the pleasures of the day they are offering. It is very helpful to understand society and its changes, in order never to be duped, and to be able to recognize what is real when you come across it. An important element, however, is strangely missing in these damaging revelations: I also like good wine and, at least in this area, I have very generally kept myself within the bounds of excess.

"But the agents of General Information and the D.S.T. do not always get proof of what Debord is up to. They suspect that with Lebovici, he finances this or that 'movement,' and that he also knows a lot of people. Continually on the alert, Debord leads the life of a recluse, always in search of someone or something. Mesrine, for example. The 'Pope' follows Mesrine's infernal path to another world. Last September, always 'accompanied' by the General Information agents, Debord leaves Arles like he does every year and goes to his country house in Bellevue-la-Montagne. Discreet, never saying hello, the Debords hide themselves. The only signs of life are late at night, say their neighbors. Cars arrive and then leave again. Quite a crowd and a fashionable crowd, insist the General Information agents who have in their possession a rather impressive list of the frequent guests and 'contacts' that are hand-picked by Debord. It is this list, these 'contacts' that will be the source of the 'other Lebovici affair.' Not the crime itself, but the aftereffects that this assassination is in the process of creating. In fact, not since the De Broglie affair[19] has the Crime Bureau or police head-quarters been subjected to such a bombardment of 'requests' and 'recommendations.' In any event, one of the 'recommendations' will demonstrate that if the Lebovici affair upsets a lot of people, it also proves the power of Debord. It has actually been 'recommended' to the chief criminal investigator that he question Guy Debord only as the last resort. And with the greatest discretion. All of which was done...three days after the assassination of Lebovici."

That is the last installment in the series. And it is obviously extremely dubious. Especially these "cars that arrive and then leave again." In such a desert, would it not be more normal that they stayed? After a while, we would have had a parking lot there, and we know now all that modern society can do with a parking lot. It is flattering to learn one day that one possesses such "power." Up to now, this has been kept hidden from me. But then, of course, power makes you many ene-mies, and more and more frequently, the enemy mur-ders you while laughing at the police. But where does this power come from and what is its nature? Perhaps it comes from knowing how to write, without any con-cessions, exactly what I think of our times. It would therefore not be anything more than the power of "strong souls over weak spirits," which already in history has been able to pass for witchcraft. It is this, namely "to pursue one's infernal path to another world," rather than one's heavenly career in this one. Obviously I do not claim to consider myself innocent, having taken certain historic responsibilities. Hegel has said that only rocks are innocent. But what is truly admirable is that no one dares to say precisely what they are reproaching me for; and that all of them pile up, not only without proof, but without any plausibility, the same stupid incriminations which can only seek to prove themselves through sheer repetition.

What a strange and unfortunate land, where one is informed of the work of an author more quickly and confidently through police archives than through the literary criticisms of a free press or through academics who make a profession out of knowing the issue at hand!

No trivial detail, you will have noticed, seems to pass by without incurring the wrath of my critics. After having insisted that I have not had a known residence for the past fifteen years or more, they draw up a list of my residences and perorate about their various styles. We have already seen that they judged the apartment that I had in Paris near Saint-Nicolas-des-Champs as luxurious. But what do they say about the others? The March 19 *Le Progrès de Lyon*[20] reveals the following: "One has even asked the question (which by the way is still unanswered) whether Gérard Lebovici had any ties or connections in the Haute-Loire. What is known is that in a small hamlet in the region Bellevue-la-Montagne, some thirty kilometers from Puy, existed and still exists two old farmhouses, consisting of several main buildings, bought a good twelve years ago by people who were among his intimate friends. Renovated and refurbished, the two large farmhouses, through the desire of its occupants, were to rapidly become places cut off from...the rest of the world—an attitude that was a sudden contrast to the friendly dealings that had presided over their moving in. Surrounded by high walls that they had rebuilt in some places, raised higher in others, only the owners' friends and intimates were permitted to enter, the mailman and gendarmes being kept away. The place especially came to life at night, from June to September, and they entertained a lot. Some powerful cars, even Rolls Royces, were parked outside the main building just last summer. Was Gérard Lebovici among those who frequented the place? That is not impossible, and moreover, it would only help complete the portrait, already shrouded in mystery, of the Parisian film agent and producer whose death is for now just as mysterious."

These two old farmhouses "existed and still exist." We can relish the laconic style, the thickly laden subtext. One would say it was something from Tacitus. But I do not doubt that they will disappear, yes they too, one of these days, those cursed farmhouses. They will be razed to the ground, and salt spread over the area. The gendarmes being kept away, this property would have signified a fraction of territory that escaped from the authority of the Republic, the height of a Langue d'oc independence movement, which would begin on a small scale, but radically. Worse than a Canak[21], I would have raised the black flag of independence—but stamped with the skull and crossbones of the pirates of old—and of course they would have let me do as I wanted. The great walls that cut the place off from the world evoke the châteaux of de Sade, a Silling in the Auvergne. Yes, Gérard Lebovici had some ties to the Haute-Loire. I like to believe that he always felt at home there. If, hypothetically, one considers that this "would only help complete the portrait, already shrouded in mystery, of the Parisian film agent and producer," only one conclusion can come from this, one that is very hostile to the economic development of this forgotten mountain region, victim of the worst storms, so often the site of natural disasters, and very imperfectly "re-integrated": if you do not desire to die prematurely, and you do not want to shroud yourself more deeply in the mystery that could be held against you, you must especially never frequent the Haute-Loire.

The March 24 *Le Provençal* [22] adds, with a sort of provincial pride: "Oh yes! Guy Debord lives in Arles. One of the inspirers of situationism, one of the master-thinkers among the May '68 protesters, a major philosopher who has provoked a change in how the consumer society is thought of...—Debord lives in an 18th century house, in the old center of Arles." And in the March 31 *Minute*: "Not really a bad situation for the 'Pope of situationism,' as he is known in leftist nomenclature! Comrade Guy Debord—who was questioned at length by the Criminal Department just after the bizarre murder of his friend Lebovici—wasn't really so broke after all.... Our hazy highbrow actually maintains, beneath an apparent parasitism, a style of life that many '68ers could well envy...has chosen to live comfortably in the least polluted part of the provinces. To do this, four years ago he gave up a luxurious apartment, near the Saint-Nicolas-des-Champs church, in order to move into lodgings in Arles that were not any less opulent.... A nice apartment, say those who live in the area, even though the doors are rarely open, except for the visitors (unfamiliar to the neighbors) that the pseudo-philosopher invites over. It should be added that Debord has the means and the connections to furnish the place according to his tastes which perhaps are not very discerning, but in any case are very expensive.... His 'bro-in-law,' a 40-year-old Eurasian, Eugene Becker-Ho, actually works in the high-class antique junk trade in Paris.... Supplied in this way with the furnishings and décor from his Parisian pieds-à-terres, Debord, who moves around a lot, spends three months every summer in his other residence at Bellevue-la-Montagne in the Haute-Loire region. After that, his brother-in-law lends him his Normandy manor house in Saint-Pierre-du-Mont...."

A photo attached to this article shows a 15th—century manor house, in fact a very beautiful one. I am familiar with the house, but it is not true that I spend part of the year there. Without being able to raise the slightest doubt when it comes to the magnificent hospitality of my brother-in-law, which can easily go as far as being extravagant, I confess that I am not so often attracted by the weather in Normandy. But after all, why is any of this my concern, even on the level of the insipid details which these journalists delight in? Unless, on top of everything, they are trying to insinuate that I married for money. Lewis Carroll would have demonstrated better than myself that, as the result of a long chain of rigorous syllogisms, the person who marries a Chinese woman from Shanghai exposes himself to the risk of having a brother-in-law who is an antique dealer in Paris. It is equally ridiculous to imagine that my apartment in Arles (whose doors "are rarely open, except for the visitors" that I invite over, which is the case, I believe, for all private apartments, even undoubtedly the office-apartment that the head curator of the Louvre museum occupies) would be furnished in a particularly expensive manner. The fact of having a brother-in-law who is an antique dealer should instead give the impression that everything becomes less expensive. Besides, everything is less costly for people who have taste. These journalists count up the centuries of my various residences. I have been more extreme than they realize: for a long time I lived in Florence in a house from the 14th century. However, the château life is not exactly my style. I have also lived comfortably among the lowest levels of society, among the Kabyles[23] in Paris, surrounded by gypsies, always in good company. In short, I have lived everywhere except among the intellectuals of this era. This is obviously because I despise them; and who then, knowing their complete works, will be surprised at this?

As we have seen, I appear on the proscription lists of my time. Everywhere else, my name has been effaced—from art, from the history of ideas, from the history of contemporary events. That does not take one ounce away from the weight of the fanatic envy of my enemies who, one may think, would also prefer to see me living in a modern condominium and eating fast-food.

The March 30 *Paris-Match* features a blurry, distant picture of me with the following text : "Who killed Gérard Lebovici? For many police officers, whether they belong to the D.S.T., to the General Information department, or to the Crime Bureau, one of the most serious trails leads to the entourage of Guy Debord, the enigmatic guru of the producer who was assassinated in the parking lot on avenue Foch, in Paris. Confidential writer, obscure filmmaker, nihilistic philosopher doubling as an avowed anti-Soviet, this fearsome agent of destablization was in contact with Italian and German intellectuals who themselves were very close to some revolutionary groups, the Red Brigades and the Baader gang.... Now that his patron Lebovici is dead,

Debord—who has already been questioned at the quai des Orfèvres 'without any results'—leads the life of a recluse in Arles, behind the shutters of his apartment. That's where *Paris-Match* caught up with him, withdrawing into his own mysterious existence. On the first floor of an 18th—century apartment building, right in the center of Arles, Guy Debord and his wife do not go out anymore. They see very few people and are perpetually on guard."

They make it seem bad, this "life of a recluse," perpetually "on guard," even though it only lasted several days and was used merely as a defense against the photographers. What serves as an opportune distraction from such a distressing affair is the amusement that one gets in preventing a swarm of photographers from achieving their mediocre goals and earning their bonuses. The layout of the terrain was rather favorable to my side. I would certainly be a bad strategist of the urban environment if I did not know how to outmaneuver photographers. Always well accompanied, I was able to go out, eat at a restaurant, wander through the city, without a single one of these clods—who are used to forcing none-too-reluctant stars out of their hiding—figuring out how to meet up with me or daring to get close enough to take a picture and get a decent image. I do not think, having watched their performances, that I was sent the cream of the profession. But what they lacked in quality they made up for in quantity, and they did not skimp on the time they took for this operation. They did not rob their bosses too much, for they were always there, on foot or in a car, every day and almost every hour. To tell the truth, almost all of them went together to have lunch and dinner, but not without leaving one or two as guards. The only strong point in their deployment of forces was the almost constant supervision of my door, and the ability to operate in packs if they had intercepted me in the street. So they had their chances.

Finally, I had pictures taken of some of them, which seemed to scare them. Everywhere, the professional underlings of the spectacle believe that they are and must be the only ones who ask the questions, who judge, who do the documenting. If the opposite happens, it demoralizes them. However, I don't mean to say that these people have personally treated me worse than anyone else; quite the opposite, it is with me that they had no success.

The March 17 *Minute* eloquently raises its conclusions to the level of the philosophy of history, which would seem to be dominated, as was first believed, by providence: "If a journalist accepts to delve into the life of this strange man, it is not out of inclination, or a morbid sense of pleasure, or perversion. It is because, when chance or providence offers such strong evidence of the validity of his fears, of the reality of a world that he has sensed and denounced for many years, of the existence of shadowy men who sap, undermine, subvert and destroy, he does not have the right to not point the finger and shout out, There he is! These types of men exist. This war that they are waging against us is indeed real. The proof.... Well? Well, if you believe in fairy tales, you will also swallow the story that it was purely accidental, namely this meeting between a bad actor born in the back of a store who provided the 'first impresario agency in Paris' and this unknown writer/obscure filmmaker, avowed anti-Soviet (to the point of hysteria), who juggles with money that he did not earn since he does not work, money from an account in a bank that is controlled by the Soviets."

I would very willingly admit that I am an obscure filmmaker in both senses of the word. But I am certainly not an "unknown writer." And since they have so much insisted on my clandestine and mysterious nature, I will take advantage of this opportunity, almost providential, to declare openly—while defying anybody to prove otherwise—that I have never published any work under a pseudonym, contrary to so many writers who sometimes agree to do a job that pays the rent, or to those who want to play at being clandestine, or even to those who for various reasons may have wanted to mystify the public. How is it possible to come to the conclusion that I do not work? For 12 years I managed and ran a journal, wrote a book and a number of smaller works–pamphlets and tracts–made and edited six films. To a great extent, during an entire generation, the work of the negative in Europe has been lead by me. I have merely refused salaried work, a career with the State, or the least subsidy from the State under whatever form that might be—and to be as clear as possible, certainly not from any foreign State—and even a simple diploma from the State, with the only and insignificant exception of a high school diploma. I do not believe that one could say in good faith that I have been continually wasting my time and amusing myself.

With these calumnies snowballing, and without a single word uttered in my defense, the newspapers would perhaps have reached the point of transforming this subject into a daily column, if I hadn't shut them up with a single blow. While on this subject, I agree that it

would not be natural to expect a word of truth or a dig-
nified gesture from a journalist of these times. But one
must not forget that today in France, besides professional journalists, there is not an historian, a philosopher, a sociologist, a marxologist, a kremlinologist, a fil-
mologist, a novelist, etc., who does not often write for a
newspaper or a weekly, and if possible for several of
them. So, in speaking of a unanimous and abetting
silence, this really concerns the entire intelligentsia. All
the same, I have to cite as an exception Iommi-
Amunatégui who alone, in *Le Matin*[24], said what almost
everyone knew to be the case. And even Régis Debray
proved to be another exception—I've been told that he
stated on television that I was not an assassin, and that
one "out of two intellectuals on the left" had read my
writings. But as Debray is always unfortunate in his
choices, he has shown that he was one of the two who
have not read my work, because he also attributed to me
a book that had been written by somebody else. I am
reminded of an observation of Orwell's in his *Homage
to Catalonia* (French translation published by Champ
Libre). He noticed that in 1937 the Stalinist newspapers, regardless of where they had been published, sys-
tematically slandered their adversaries without even the
slightest moderation, except in England: "The reason,
of course, is simply that several sharp lessons have given

the English Communist press a wholesome dread of the law of libel."

I have always disregarded the press. I have never been tempted to exercise the right to reply, and even less still would I have wanted to try to take legal action against people who have been defaming me as far back as I can remember. But they had never said before that I had assassinated, or had someone assassinate, a friend. They were wrong to go that far. I found this instance so exceptional that I made an exception. I therefore sued several newspapers for libel. All of them instantly stopped making the slightest insinuation of this kind. Subsequently, I naturally won, or rather my lawyer won the libel cases as they came up. The defamers were ordered to pay me a certain amount of money, and in addition to have published at their expense each one of these libel judgments in three newspapers of my choice. But I do not wish to choose any newspaper, finding them all of equal value. I do not have a better opinion of their readers, and I am not interested in rectifying their reports on me. The only thing that I could not allow this time was to let them say whatever they wanted.

The March 29 *Libération* describes this action of mine in the following terms: "Guy Debord is suing the *Journal du Dimanche* for libel. Since the assassination of

Gérard Lebovici, who was his friend, his publisher and the producer of his last two films, the name of Guy Debord has appeared in two articles in the *Journal du Dimanche* which implied that his (evil) influence was, directly or indirectly, the cause of the producer's assassination. Guy Debord, one of the founders of the Situationist International, which dissolved itself in 1969, was called, among other polite names, Lebovici's 'angel of darkness' and 'a third-rate Mephistopheles in a real tragedy: that of the bewitchment of a man.' Other actions are being contemplated against *Minute* and *L'Humanité*. Still, one is surprised that the situationist Debord places any kind of confidence in the judicial system, even one that is temporary, dictated by circumstances and a friendship cut short."

I am not any more of a situationist than any other. I was a situationist during the whole time that the S.I. lasted, and I congratulate myself for that. I wrote in 1960, in number 4 of the Situationist International journal: "There is no 'situationism.' I myself am only a situationist by the fact of my participation, in this moment and under certain conditions, in a community that has come together for practical reasons with a certain task in sight, which it will know how or not know how to accomplish." (Since 1968 I have thought that essentially it did know how.)

It is well known that the Situationist International came to an end 12 years ago; that is why these people have allowed themselves to write such audacious lies. What would the situationists have done in the face of such provocations? In referring to some examples from our past, I suppose that they simply would have beaten the first slanderers with a stick, in public and on the same day that their articles appeared; and in this way, it would not have been necessary to return a sense of reality to more than four or five of these individuals, for after that nobody would have wanted to expose himself to such insult.

The newspaper *Libération* seems to think that my opinions, past and present, have placed me in the position of being the only one in France who is in some way outside the protection of all its laws; and that if, for example, some real estate owners had the sudden whim to submit to the courts a kind of greedy, self-serving interpretation of the conditions of certain leases, I would have to be obligated to not defend myself in such a situation, and therefore to give in to them. Of course, nobody is so stupid as to believe this. Still, one pretends to be surprised. In the same way, one pretends, as if this were an everyday euphemism, to call "a friendship cut short" what is in fact a premeditated assassination by ambush.

These journalists—each one slavishly readapting every startling discovery of whomever else, with, however, a certain undeniable collective verve—have called me (without ever tying their description to any corresponding fact): Mastermind, nihilist, pseudo-philosopher, Pope, loner, mentor, hypnotizer, bloodstained stooge, fanatic of himself, devil, éminence grise, damned soul, Professor of Radicalism, guru, secondhand revolutionary, agent of subversion and destablization in the pay of Soviet imperialism, third-rate Mephistopheles, noxious, eccentric, hazy, enigmatic, angel of darkness, ideologue, mystery man, mad sadist, complete cynic, the dregs of non-thought, bewitcher, fearsome destabilizer, enragé, theoretician.

Among such a cartload, I accept the last two names: "theoretician," that goes without saying, although I have not practiced that exclusively nor with a specialized title, but in the end I have been one as well, and one of the best. And I also accept "enragé," because in 1968 I acted in concert with the extremists who at the time gave themselves that name; and in addition because I have an affinity for those of 1794. I could abstractly accept "fearsome destabilizer" if this description did not immediately have the connotation of terrorist and even someone in the pay of a foreign State. All the other descriptions are exactly the opposite of who I am, and have almost always been chosen exactly because of that. A society that polemicizes in this way must have many things to hide. And as we know, this one does.

When the entire storehouse of knowledge, taste and language that is available to experts of this kind will be stored on disks of artificial memory, we will see what can be learned at the computer. Very soon, the judgments to be rendered in Newspeak will resemble in each instance the one that was inaugurated with me in this affair. One wonders how a computer will be able to translate the word "nobility" in a few years.

Gérard Lebovici had published many more classics than works of contemporary subversives, but in a time of decadence and programmed ignorance, where the revolution that is rising is detected less than the society that is falling, even the publication of classics passes for a subversive act.

Guy Debord

The April 7-8 *Le Soir*[25] of Brussels maintains that the Situationist International has succeeded to an extraordinary extent, meets with general admiration at this time, has changed all of this era's ideas, and that none of this was really worth the bother, since all revolutions basically are circular—one always ends up being recuperated, and in the end it is always a mistake to revolt. They cite what happened to Gérard Lebovici as an example of the profound irony of history, where each person must change roles, with fatal consequences. I myself would play a curious role, in order to correspond to this circular schema: "One shudders to imagine the dramatic event on avenue Foch as the inexorable fulfill-ment of a logic that is dreadful even in its irony, a logic that is inherent in certain destinies. Following the pro-gression of a terrifying circularity, it is at the moment that the revolutionary, who had made it a profession to 'live dangerously,' attains security and peace, that the 'established man' who supplies the funds meets his trag-ic end at the turnstile of an underground parking lot on avenue Foch. It is not even impossible that at the heart of this labyrinth from which he would never again find the exit, the last thing crossing the mind of the produc-er and patron Gérard Lebovici was this Latin palin-drome which, turning indefinitely onto itself in such a way that the end reverses identically into the beginning, was the title of the last film of Debord advertised for the cinema Cujas: *In girum imus nocte et consumimur igni.* ('We turn around and around in darkness and are consumed by fire.')"

I am completely sure that I have never in any way attained security and peace, certainly now less than ever. The prevailing falsity and charlatanry of this world will always be able to gain the approval of each and everyone, but it will have to do without mine.

That everything ends in success, concessions and the shabby rewards of success, is exactly what is contradicted by the history of hundreds of revolutionary attempts here and there. In any case, that kind of success cannot be applied to the Situationist International. The S.I. itself knew how to fight its own glory, just as it had predicted it would. This practice is almost unprecedented. The S.I. did not want to become a commandment for anyone, and it did not even want to prolong itself as a kind of intellectual authority for future days. We had nothing for ourselves but time. When I talk of myself, which I have done rarely, a certain peremptory tone surfaces, which is indeed appropriate but often disapproved of, although that is not too surprising. Many others do not have recourse to this, because they have to observe the formalities, and also lack the content. It is beautiful to have contributed to the ruination of this world. What other success did we deserve to have?

I do not think that I am as "enigmatic" as they like to say. I even believe that I am at times easy to understand. Not too long ago, in the first stages of a passion, the woman with whom I was talking to of the brief periods of exile that we had both known, said to me, in that tone of noble abruptness which goes so well in Spain: "But you, you have spent all of your life in exile."

So I have had the pleasures of exile, as others have had the pains of submission. Gérard Lebovici was assassinated.

(January 1985)

1. Jacques Mesrine. See Introduction, page i.

2. *France-Soir*: a daily newspaper, targeting middle-brow readers.

3. *Rivarol*: an extreme right-wing weekly newspaper.

4. *L'Humanité*: official daily newspaper of the French communist party.

5. *Minute*: right-wing daily newspaper.

6. *Le Nouvel Observateur*: a weekly magazine of the pro-Socialist variety.

7. For more details and analysis of the Italian government's manipulation of the Red Brigades and other terrorist organizations during the 1970s, as well as its subsequent involvement in the kidnapping and murder of Aldo Moro, see Guy Debord's "Preface to the Fourth Italian Edition of the The Society of the Spectacle", published in the same edition of his *Commentaries on the Society of the Spectacle*. Equally enlightening is *On Terrorism and the State* by Gianfranco Sanguinetti. Sanguinetti is the same man who wrote a report detailing the Italian government's involvement in the Piazza Fontana bombing, published it under the pseudonym of Censor and passed it off as the disclosures of a man with the highest government contacts. The Italian press and public was completely taken in.

8. *Présent*: an extreme right-wing daily newspaper.

9. Captain Barril: A former soldier and security expert that President Mitterand promoted to a position of superagent to fight terrorism during the 1980s.

10. Maspero: defunct marxist-leninist-trotskyite publishers from the '60s and '70s who published particularly pitiful books on the left. Debord and the situationists turned it into a verb, signifying the misappropriation and butchering of a text.

11. *Le Journal du Dimanche*: the only French national newspaper published on Sundays.

12. *VSD*: stands for Vendredi, Samedi, Dimanche (Friday, Saturday, Sunday). A

glossy weekly magazine full of current affairs and celebrity gossip, similar to *Paris-Match*.

13. *Tout sur le Personnage*: literally, Everything about the Person. The book was posthumously published by Éditions Gérard Lebovici in 1984.

14. *Le Point*: a weekly magazine that covers politics, current affairs, business, etc.; it has a slightly liberal bent.

15. *Le Quotidien* de Paris: a daily newspaper, similar to *France-Soir*.

16. D.S.T.: Direction de la Surveillance du Territoire, equivalent to British MI5 or to the American C.I.A.

17. General Information: Renseignments Généraux, security branch of the French police force. It is under the French Minister of the Interior and is the equivalent to the F.B.I.

18. *Libération*: left-leaning daily newspaper.

19. The de Broglie affair: Prince Jean de Broglie, Gaullist member of the French Parliament who was mysteriously shot dead on 24 December 1976.

20. *Le Progrès de Lyon*: another lower-middle-brow daily newspaper for the Rhone-Alpes region of France.

21. Canak: indigenous people of New Caledonia who first revolted against French rule in 1878, and re-organized in 1984 with the formation of Front de Liberation Nationale Kanak Socialiste (FLNKS). The French government has repeatedly acted to suppress any independence movement.

22. *Le Provençal*: a Socialist daily newspaper for Marseille.

23. Kabyles: people from the mountainous region of Algeria.

24. *Le Matin*: a Socialist-leaning daily newspaper.

25. *Le Soir*: a Belgian daily national newspaper, equivalent to *Le Monde*.

BOOKS

TamTam Book Series